Authors
Kids Love

Joseph Bruchac

An Author Kids Love

by Michelle Parker-Rock

Enslow Elementary

an imprint of

Enslow Publishers, Inc.

 40 Industrial Road
Box 398
Berkeley Heights, NJ 07922
USA

http://www.enslow.com

This book is based on a live interview with Joseph Bruchac on June 6, 2007.

For my grandparents, S., H., R., and M, and my parents, B., and L.,
who live on in our stories. And to J.B., heartfelt thanks.—Olakamigenoka.
May we all live in peace.

Enslow Elementary, an imprint of Enslow Publishers, Inc.

Enslow Elementary® is a registered trademark of Enslow Publishers, Inc.

Library of Congress Cataloging-in-Publication Data

Parker-Rock, Michelle.
    Joseph Bruchac : an author kids love / Michelle Parker-Rock.
        p. cm. — (Authors kids love)
    "Based on a live interview with Joseph Bruchac on June 6, 2007"—T.p. verso.
    Includes bibliographical references and index.
    Summary: "Explores the life of author Joseph Bruchac, including his childhood and early career, his many books for kids, and tips he has for young, aspiring writers"—Provided by publisher.
    ISBN-13: 978-0-7660-3160-9
    ISBN-10: 0-7660-3160-8
    1. Bruchac, Joseph, 1942– —Juvenile literature. 2. Bruchac, Joseph, 1942– —Interviews—Juvenile literature. 3. Authors, American—20th century—Biography—Juvenile literature. 4. Indian authors—United States—Biography—Juvenile literature. 5. Abenaki Indians—Biography—Juvenile literature. 6. Children's stories—Authorship—Juvenile literature. I. Title.
    PS3552.R794Z84 2009
    818'.5409—dc22
    [B]   2008033051

Printed in the United States of America

10 9 8 7 6 5 4 3 2 1

To Our Readers: We have done our best to make sure that all Internet Addresses in this book were active and appropriate when we went to press. However, the author and publisher have no control over and assume no liability for the material available on those Internet sites or on other Web sites they may link to. Any comments or suggestions can be sent by e-mail to comments@enslow.com or to the address on the back cover.

♻ Enslow Publishers, Inc., is committed to printing our books on recycled paper. The paper in every book contains 10% to 30% post-consumer waste (PCW). The cover board on the outside of each book contains 100% PCW. Our goal is to do our part to help young people and the environment too!

Photo Credits: Courtesy of Joseph Bruchac, pp. 3, 7, 9, 12, 14, 16, 21, 23, 30, 33; Michelle Parker-Rock © 2007, pp. 1, 3 (bottom), 4, 32, 43, 44, 47.

Cover Photo: Front cover, © Michelle Parker-Rock 2007; back cover, courtesy of Joseph Bruchac.

Contents

Chapter 1 Our Blood Is All Red 5

Chapter 2 Looking and Listening 11

Chapter 3 Little Seeds 20

Chapter 4 Turkey Brother and Thirteen Moons 29

Chapter 5 Gah-neh-go-hi-yo: The Good Mind 34

Chapter 6 Ktsi Nwaskw: Great Spirit 41

Selected Books by Joseph Bruchac 45

Words to Know 46

Further Reading and Internet Addresses .. 47

Index 48

Our Blood Is All Red

In Joseph Bruchac's story "The Gift of Stories, The Gift of Breath," a little girl asks her grandfather where stories come from. "Stories are all around us," he tells her. "They're inside us, too. They're like our breath." The little girl asks her grandfather if she has stories in her. "You do," he says. "Just keep looking, and sometimes, like on those mornings when you can see your breath, you'll see them. Just keep listening, and you'll hear them, as you do that little wind that is blowing now."

Joseph Bruchac has spent a lifetime looking and listening. He listened to stories told by his family,

5

friends, teachers, and Native elders, and he looked deep within himself and his Abenaki roots, once a family secret, to understand his Indian heritage and discover the stories he was meant to tell. He has worked to preserve the language, music, skills and tales of the Abenaki culture, and he shares these traditions around the world through his award-winning books and storytelling.

Joseph Bruchac was born on October 16, 1942, in Greenfield Center, a little town near the Adirondack Mountains in New York. His great-grandparents on his mother's side, Ed and Flora Dunham, were of English descent, from a family they said could be traced back to the *Mayflower*. The Dunhams had a hired hand named Jesse Bowman, who fell in love with their daughter, Marion Flora. It angered the Dunhams, because Bowman was a dark-skinned laborer with no formal education. To keep Bowman away from Marion Flora, the Dunhams sent her to stay with her brother in Virginia. Bowman followed her there, and eventually they married and moved to a house in Greenfield Center, where Bruchac's mother, Flora Marion, was born.

Bruchac's father, Joseph Bruchac Jr., was the son of Slovak immigrants. In Slovakia, the Bruchacs were woodsmen and hunters. During the Great Depression of the 1930s, when many people were unemployed and poor, Joseph Jr. hunted, trapped, and sold animal skins to help support his family. He also took up the trade of taxidermy, the art of stuffing and mounting dead animals for display.

Joseph Jr. and Flora married and had three children: Joe; Mary Ann, born two years after Joe; and Margaret, born eleven years later. For the first few years, Joe's parents shared a house on the corner of Middle Grove Road and Route 9N with Jesse and Marion. When Joe was three, the Bowmans gave his parents a nearby house on ninety acres. Joe remained with his grandparents while Mary Ann moved to the new house with their parents.

Joseph Bruchac's grandmother, Marion Flora Dunham Bowman.

Abenaki Indians

The Abenaki (ah-ben-AH-kee), whose name means "Dawn Land," are one of the original Native peoples of northern New England. In addition to those residing on two reserves in Canada, there are thousands of Abenaki people today living in many parts of northern New York, Vermont, and New Hampshire.

The Abenakis hunted, fished, trapped, and grew corn, beans, and squash. Saratoga Springs, New York, is one of the places where Abenaki artisans would sell their baskets, leatherwork, beadwork, and other crafts. Many traditional Abenaki stories feature a trickster raccoon, as in *Raccoon's Last Race: A Traditional Abenaki Story* by Joseph Bruchac and his son James.

Joseph Bruchac

Jesse and Marion Bowman owned and operated a general store and the Splinterville Hill Filling Station, known to most as "Bowman's Store." Joe seldom spent time with his parents, except when they went for car rides on the weekends or to dinners at the home of his paternal grandparents, Joseph Bruchac and Pauline Hrdlicka.

Bruchac explained:

The idea was, as my grandmother put it, to make ends meet. It was the 1940s, during World War II. My grandparents were helping my parents by sharing the raising of the children. All I knew was that I was not with

8

my mom and dad. I also knew that my dad had a bad temper and I think my grandparents were trying to protect me from him. I remember coming back from a Sunday drive with my parents with a big red mark across my face where my father had slapped me. I was very upset, but my grandfather said, "You're safe with us."

At one point, Bruchac's father demanded that his grandparents give him back, but they refused.

When Bruchac was growing up, many Native people, including his grandfather Jesse, kept their ethnicity a secret because of the prejudice against them. "There are some very dark-skinned people in the photo albums of the Dunham family that nobody talked about," he said. "I am sure there was Native ancestry there." Even though he was unaware of

Joe as a baby with his parents, Joseph and Flora Bruchac.

his own Abenaki roots at the time, the young Bruchac found himself drawn to American Indian culture. Over time, he came to see that his father had been attracted to it as well. As a child, Joseph Jr.'s favorite book was Ernest Thompson Seton's *Two Little Savages*, a story about two boys who lived like Indians, and his first partner in taxidermy was Leon Pray, an Ottawa Indian, who remained his lifelong friend. Eventually Bruchac came to see how the different branches of his ancestry came from similar roots.

There are many things we human beings have in common, but we forget because of cultural differences. This is not to lessen the importance of those different languages, stories, and traditions that have been built up over centuries or thousands of years, but I think that beneath it all, there is that old teaching that Native elders have given me. Our blood is all red. Our breath is all the same and shared with the same wind. We have deep connections, and I think that is very important to recognize.

Looking and Listening

Bruchac was aware that people often made remarks about his dark-skinned grandfather, but he did not understand why. "It confused me," he said. He knew that people in the community regarded him differently, too, because he was poor and wore shirts that his grandmother made out of floral-patterned feedsacks. When he asked his grandfather if he was Native American, Bowman never gave a direct answer.

He told me that he only went as far as fourth grade in school because the kids kept calling him a dirty Indian. When he could not stand it any longer, he jumped out the window and never went back.

Jesse Bowman holds his grandson Joe.

He said he didn't like being called a dirty Indian. That in itself was denial, but it was actually a confirmation. I just didn't realize it at the time.

Bowman told people he was French because it was safer than admitting who he was. His great-grandfather had come to the United States from an Abenaki Indian Reserve in French-speaking Canada to serve in the Civil War. But during the middle of the twentieth century, Indians were not regarded as noble. More often, they were considered inferior, or people who no longer existed. Bruchac said:

All the images tended to be stereotypes. Movies, television, and most books showed American Indian people as lower than second-class citizens. I remember when I was in college, and I actually looked at an encyclopedia entry from a book published in Europe that described the Abenakis as an extinct American Indian people. They no longer existed. That sort of backdrop is what I was operating against.

While living with his grandfather, Bruchac experienced many things about being Abenaki. "I learned about being quiet and about listening," he said, "and I learned to respect the natural world. If I caught a fish I'd say thank you to the fish for letting me catch it."

Bowman used stories to enlighten his grandson. "That way of teaching is very Abenaki," said Bruchac. "His quietness and his great ability to listen prepared me for finding my way into a culture that I really didn't know I knew anything about."

His grandparents were also generous. They allowed customers at their general store to pay for their purchases at a later time. They also loaned money to people, even though they did not have much for themselves. Indian families would bring the game they hunted to the store, and Bowman would sell it and give them the money without taking any money for himself. "I remember my grandmother selling vegetables that her nephew had grown in his garden. If she sold a dollar's worth of vegetables, she gave him a dollar. It was regarded as the right way to behave," he said.

Jesse Bowman could barely read or write. "He wrote me letters when I was in college," said Bruchac. "Most of it was *I miss you, I love you*, and Xs and Os." His grandmother, on the other hand, was a graduate of Skidmore College and Albany Law School. She passed the bar exam (a test to become a lawyer), but she never actually practiced law beyond writing wills and deeds for people. At one point, she was the town clerk and a member of the school board. "She was very influential in her ways," Bruchac said. "She was determined to do what she believed in and was committed to the welfare of people."

She also taught Bruchac to read.

Bruchac enjoyed animals and nature from the time he was a very young child.

14

"I remember breaking through with my ABCs," he said, "and how wonderful it was when the words finally took shape on the page. I realized there were stories there and that I could read them." At the library in Saratoga Springs, Bruchac found *Babar*, *Charlotte's Web*, *Uncle Wiggily*, and *A Child's Garden of Verses*. At home, there were bookshelves everywhere, filled with hundreds of books, including the works of Shakespeare and Dickens. "Suddenly, I was reading Kipling's *The Jungle Book* and Stevenson's *Treasure Island* in second and third grade by myself," he said. He also enjoyed some of the popular series, like the Tom Swift, Bobbsey Twins, and Tarzan books, and he loved comics and books about nature, too. "I remember reading *Bring 'Em Back Alive* by Frank Buck, as well as the bird books by Roger Tory Peterson and the work of naturalist Edwin Way Teal," he said. "I thought I might become a naturalist, and maybe I'd end up in a national park working as a ranger or a nature interpreter, educating others about the natural world."

Bruchac loved animals. There were always dogs,

cats, frogs, toads, rabbits, salamanders, and snakes around Bowman's store. One time, Bruchac ordered flying squirrels for $5.95 from a comic book ad. "When the box arrived, I imagined finding these cute tame creatures inside. Instead, two little things exploded out of the box and disappeared in the house. I never saw them again."

In second grade, Bruchac wrote a poem for his teacher. She read it to the class and praised him, but the kids teased him and beat him up. "I didn't have a label for myself," he said, "but I knew that I was the smallest kid in the class with big glasses. I was always getting picked on." As early as third grade, Bruchac enjoyed writing essays. "Writing came easily," he said. "I was thinking I'd be a writer-naturalist and write about animals, just like the authors I was reading."

As a child, Joe enjoyed making his classmates laugh.

Although Bruchac was not a popular kid, he could get his

16

classmates to laugh because he could write things that were funny. "If anything, I viewed myself as a kind of bookish coward," he said. "I was like the kid who knew too much." He had a flair for theatrics, too. "This is how I got attention and approval from the other kids. I was the guy who could be the ham. In that way, I could stand out, make people laugh, and be accepted to some degree, despite my differences."

During his junior and senior years at Saratoga High School, Bruchac worked as a counselor at a camp called Skye Farm, where he pursued his interest in becoming a naturalist. In school, he excelled in English and social studies, and he composed a winning essay for a "Speak for Democracy" contest. He also received praise from his classmates for his original stories.

When Bruchac was seventeen, his grandmother died. Both he and his grandfather experienced deep grief. That same year, Bruchac went through a major physical transformation, growing half a foot. At almost six feet two inches tall, he went from being a bookworm to being a jock. He became a shot putter and discus thrower for the track team, a varsity heavyweight wrestler, and the right tackle on the football team. "At the time, being an athlete was more important to me in terms of identity than my ethnicity," he said.

One Sunday, after a football game, Bruchac was surprised to see his parents sitting in the stands. Shortly after, his father invited him to go pheasant hunting. On one of their outings, Bruchac's father told him that his grandfather Jesse was an Abenaki Indian. That was all he ever said about it.

As high school graduation drew near, Bruchac decided he wanted to go to college. He scored very high on his high school exams and won a scholarship, which surprised many people, because by his senior year, he was not paying much attention to academics. "I was lousy in math," he said, "but I was still getting 90s and 100s in social studies and English."

While Bruchac's grandmother had always thought he would go to college, his grandfather did not even know what a college was. His own parents did nothing to encourage him. "In fact," he said, "my father made the comment that he didn't think I could survive in college. He didn't think I could do it. He knew very little about me."

Nonetheless, Bruchac applied to Cornell University's College of Agriculture to study wildlife conservation. He later learned that the essay he sent with his application was the reason he was accepted. "I wrote such an intelligent, sensitive essay about how I wanted to be a writer-naturalist and how Cornell was the perfect place for me to do this," he said.

Bruchac entered Cornell University in 1960. "I had no experience and I still had a terrible wardrobe," he said. "I was starting all over again, a different person in a different place, learning a lot about myself."

Chapter 3

Little Seeds

Bruchac did not expect to find prejudice and discrimination in college. In high school, many of his friends were African American, Irish American, and Jewish. "I never thought of them as being that different," he said. He often went to dance and listen to music in the part of town where many of his African-American classmates lived.

Now that I think about it, I was usually the only person in the group who would have been called white, but I didn't think of it in those terms in those days. Then I went to college and the difference was made clear to me.

Bruchac's high school graduation picture

In Bruchac's freshman year at Cornell, his grandfather came to visit. He brought with him two of Bruchac's best friends from home. Bruchac said:

He introduced them to all the kids in my dormitory as my brothers. Tommy Furlong was Irish American and David Phillips was African American. People looked at them, they looked at me, and they looked at my brown-skinned grandfather. Needless to say, it made them wonder.

That same year, Bruchac became interested in joining a fraternity. There were more than fifty of these social clubs on campus, but only three invited Bruchac to visit.

I think word had gotten around that this guy, Joe Bruchac, was part African American, having seen my grandfather and David. My grandfather thought it was very funny. He was not prejudiced the way many people were. Nor was I, for that matter. But I think of that to this day as an example of how color has transformed our culture and how it has injured people by causing them to see things in an intolerant way.

During his second year at Cornell, Bruchac took his first writing course. "I began to think of myself as a poet and a writer, rather than just as a naturalist," he said. Eventually, he became disappointed with Cornell's wildlife conservation program, and in his junior year, he transferred to Cornell's College of Arts and Sciences to focus on his writing. He also met his first girlfriend, Carol Worthen, who became his wife on June 13, 1964.

At Cornell, Bruchac's interest in his American Indian heritage intensified. He wrote poems about Native American people and had his first piece published in the Cornell literary magazine, *The Trojan Horse*, where he later became an editor.

After graduating from Cornell with a bachelor of arts degree in English and wildlife zoology, Bruchac accepted a full scholarship to Syracuse University to study fiction writing. That year, the university hired a new instructor, who strongly disapproved of Bruchac's writing. Bruchac said:

> I was so distressed by the end of the semester that I burned everything I'd written in a fire and smashed my typewriter. Then I went and bought another typewriter and a sheaf of paper and started writing again. It was 1965.

Bruchac writing in college

Halfway through the year, the famous writer Grace Paley joined the faculty of Syracuse University. She told Bruchac to write from his heart. With Paley's support, he wrote a novel entitled *One Last Summer*, about the Vietnam War. "The main character was American Indian," said Bruchac. "He was the old version of me, dealing with being Indian but not knowing much about it and trying to find his heritage at the same time he was resisting a war he didn't believe in."

Bruchac often rode his motorcycle out to the nearby Onondaga Reservation, where he would sit around talking with the Native elders.

I would listen, trying to find out whatever they wanted to share with me. I had learned as a child, growing up with my grandparents, that if you are quiet, people will talk to you. I didn't realize how much that was a part of Native culture, that idea of listening and being ready to hear. It served me well all through my life because I discovered wherever I traveled that if I just sat and listened, the elders, whether they be American Indian or African or European, were often eager to share the things they knew and the stories they had learned.

24

Bruchac began to link his young adult experiences with those of his youth. "One of the reasons my parents took us on road trips was so that my father could sell his stuffed mounted animals, but we would go for pleasure, too," he said. At Frontier Town in upstate New York there there was an Indian village run by Swift Eagle, an American Indian of Pueblo Apache ancestry.

> I would always break away from my parents and go listen to Swifty tell traditional Iroquois and Pueblo stories. He didn't know who I was then, but later on, I reconnected with him through his son Powhatan, who was a close friend of mine.

Bruchac's family also went to Indian Village at Lake George, where Ray Fadden, a Mohawk elder and an Iroquois storyteller, would tell stories and demonstrate crafts. "I had no idea who he was then, but later in life, he became a teacher and a friend of mine." Bruchac's family also visited the Enchanted Forest in Old Forge, New York. There, Maurice Dennis, who was Abenaki, would tell stories and talk about Native culture. He also became Bruchac's friend and teacher.

All of these little seeds were planted in my childhood. They connected me to the Native people in the Adirondacks, all of whom were "playing Indians" at tourist attractions, the one place where Native people could be visible in white American culture in those days.

Years later, after his father's death, Bruchac looked through his dad's journals. He recalled:

He bought a journal every year. Sometimes he wrote nothing in them. But in a journal dated 1954, he had written the name and address of Alice Papineau, a clan mother of the Onondaga Nation, whose Indian name was Dewasentah. She was, by then, a very dear friend that I had known since my college days. I had no idea she knew my father. Over time, a lot of circles reconnected.

In the fall of 1966, after graduating from Syracuse University with a master's degree in literature and creative writing, Bruchac and his wife went to Ghana to work in a program called Teachers for West Africa. "I had a lifelong fascination with Africa," he said, "because of its natural environment. I also had a fascination with African culture."

Bruchac taught in a small secondary school, and Carol ran the school's bookstore and library.

He said:

We had been in Africa for a while and realized that many of the black African kids I was teaching reminded us of the white kids we knew back home. What was interesting was that we were seeing beyond the color of their faces. We saw the person not the color of their skin, and we knew the people there were seeing us that way, too. We found ourselves amazed at how narrowly people in the United States defined humanity and how small their view of the world often is. There are so many wonderful things about American culture, but there is also this feeling of superiority. It's a really dangerous thing. It was a very important experience for me.

During their second year in Ghana, the Bruchacs' first son, Jim, was born. After three years, the Bruchacs returned to the United States and moved in with Bruchac's grandfather, circling back to Bowman's Store. A year later, Jesse Bowman died, and Bruchac grieved once more.

While he was in Ghana, Bruchac wrote a lot

of poetry and thought about publishing. At home, he and Carol started a literary magazine called *The Greenfield Review* and a small publishing company called The Greenfield Review Press. They featured writers that were Native American, African, Asian, and members of other ethnic minorities. "We published multicultural literature before people thought of multicultural literature," he said.

His first book of poetry, *Indian Mountain*, was published in 1971. The following year, the Bruchac's second son, Jesse, was born. By 1974, Bruchac had earned his doctoral degree in comparative literature at the Union Institute of Ohio. Years later, in 1983, he put together an important collection of American Indian poetry called *Songs from This Earth on Turtle's Back*. "It is still used in schools and colleges," he said. Then he left Skidmore College, where he had been teaching and writing, and he became a full-time storyteller and writer.

Turkey Brother and Thirteen Moons

$\mathcal{N}$ow that he had two sons, Bruchac began to spend more time with his parents. He wanted Jim and Jesse to know their grandparents, and he also wanted them to know their Indian heritage. Bruchac believed that storytelling was a good way to communicate the things he cared about. He said:

Storytelling became part of our regular routine. I would tell them stories I had heard and learned over the years from the various elders I had listened to in Frontier Town and the Indian Village. By then, I had reconnected with Swift Eagle and Ray Fadden, and I was hearing the same stories again as an adult that I heard as a kid. Now, I was telling them

It was important to Bruchac to tell his sons about their heritage. Here he is shown whittling.

to my kids. I wasn't writing them down or memorizing them consciously. I was just telling them as I remembered them, measuring their effectiveness by how my sons heard them.

Around that time, Bruchac's poems appeared in a magazine called *New American and Canadian Poetry*. One day, Bruchac's friend John Gill, the editor of Crossing Press, said he noticed what a great relationship Bruchac had with Jim and Jesse. Bruchac told Gill about the traditional Abenaki and Iroquois stories that he was telling his boys. Gill offered to publish the stories in a children's book, and Bruchac agreed to give it a try. He asked Jesse to repeat the stories to see if he had understood them.

I wrote them down as he was telling them to me. Then I rewrote them and gave them to John. After a few more revisions, *Turkey Brother and Other Iroquois Stories*, my first book for children, was published in 1975. A year and half later, Crossing Press published a second book of Iroquois stories called *Stone Giants and Flying Heads*. The stories in those two books, plus a few new stories, were put together and turned into a book called *Heroes and Heroines, Monsters and Magic: Native American Legends and Folktales*.

Bruchac's Mohawk friend Jon Kahionhes Fadden illustrated *Turkey Brother and Other Iroquois Stories*, as well as *Keepers of the Earth*, a series of books Bruchac wrote with Michael Caduto. The books teach about natural science through traditional American Indian stories.

Bruchac's first picture book, *Thirteen Moons on Turtle's Back,* was with Philomel Books, a major publisher. It was the result of years of correspondence with his friend Jonathan London, who was working on a book about the cycles of the moon. Many Native people used the thirteen horny scales on a turtle's back as a way to track these cycles. They also associated a story with each new moon.

Every time I wrote to Jonathan, I always dated my letters with the names of the moons. I had been working on poems about American Indians when Jonathan asked me to be his coauthor. Thomas Locker, a fine artist, did the illustrations.

Bruchac uses music and storytelling to share his traditions with audiences.

When the book was released, Bruchac was invited to read it to students at an elementary school near Ithaca, New York.

When I got in front of the class, I looked at the book, and I looked at the kids. Then I put the book down, and I said, "Let me tell you the stories." That was my first public storytelling experience.

Bruchac involved the audience with songs and a technique known as call and response, where the listeners repeat a word or a phrase that is called out. Bruchac said:

My own storytelling has been out there for so long, I have influenced other storytellers. I actually see where my influence comes in. Someone will tell a story and use a term or phrase that I know is mine. However, while a story may change and grow, it still remains true to what it is. Stories are alive. Traditionally it is said, that when you are not telling them, they tell themselves to each other.

Jim and Jesse see the purpose and the place of story in their lives, and they have followed in their father's footsteps. Both of them are storytellers and writers, and this pleases Bruchac. "Neither one of them were told or encouraged to do this. It happened naturally," he said. "I am very proud of them."

Bruchac believes that the best stories—whether they are written down or spoken—serve at least two purposes. They entertain, and they teach things that are morally and practically useful. "All I want to do is tell a good story," he said, "and my favorite story is always the one I'm telling when I'm telling it."

Jesse Bruchac. Joseph Bruchac is proud that both of his sons are storytellers and writers.

Gah-neh-go-hi-yo: The Good Mind

Bruchac's work reflects his extensive knowledge of Native American culture as well as his passion for the American Indian peoples and their stories. Accuracy is important to him because as a boy, he saw Indians wrongly portrayed in the movies as feathered fools on horseback, whooping and hollering, riding circles around a wagon train, attacking—or running away when the chief got shot.

> These were caricatures—exaggerations of Native people. I have Native friends who grew up on reservations. When they were children, they didn't think of themselves as Indians. They'd see these

34

movies and they'd identify with the cowboys. It was traumatic and emotionally upsetting for them to realize they were one of those idiots on horseback. Even people who grew up in a Native community with a deep awareness of their culture were in the same kind of denial that my grandfather was because the image of Native people in this country and the historical treatment of them were so bad.

From the late 1800s to the middle of the twentieth century, many Native American children were taken away from their homes and put into boarding schools. They were not allowed to speak their language and were told that their customs and traditions were wrong. It created a generation of people who were raised by the state. A Mohawk elder told Bruchac that his grandfather was unable to hug his grandchildren because at the boarding school he had learned to be strict with them. Bruchac said:

> There is so much that has to be undone in our generation. When I write for young people, I want them to recognize who they are, to see the good in every culture, and to see the complexity of

humanity in full and not just in a narrow little picture.

Some of Bruchac's books, like *The Circle of Thanks* and *Pushing Up the Sky*, are collections of poems, plays, and traditional stories from different Native American cultures. Other books, including *Foot of the Mountain and Other Stories*, draw specifically on his own Abenaki heritage. Bruchac's historical novels, such as *The Arrow Over the Door*, *Children of the Longhouse*, and *The Winter People* realistically show young Native characters in gripping tales about identity and survival. He said:

> I am always meeting myself in my own fiction, in both the good and the bad characters. I think my own experiences shape the people I create. For example, I feel a lot of closeness to the boy in *Geronimo*, even though he is a Chiricahua Apache, which is different from me. I feel close to him because of his relationship to Geronimo, who is his grandfather—the grandfather who went through great difficulty but remained strong.

Hidden Roots is a novel about a boy who discovers the Native ancestry of his family. "The main character, Walter, is built around me in a lot of ways," said Bruchac, "and the old man in the story is built around my grandfather in some ways." In *The Way,* the main character is deeply involved in martial arts, a discipline Bruchac has been studying for over thirty-four years.

When Bruchac writes about other cultures, he does extensive research. For *Sacajawea,* he read every page of the Lewis and Clark journals and many other books about the period. He even visited the places that Lewis and Clark explored. To understand the Shoshone, Bruchac turned to the Native people for information.

The idea for *Code Talker* came after Bruchac met some of the Navajo Marines who served the United States during World War II. He interviewed the men and consulted a Navajo expert to make sure he had used the Navajo language correctly.

For *Eagle Song,* a novel about a boy growing up in a poor Brooklyn neighborhood where Mohawk steel workers lived when they built the World Trade Center, Bruchac listened to Native kids talk about their lives in New York City.

Code Talkers

During World War II, the United States was at war with Japan. To prevent the Japanese from finding out their battle plans, the Americans used secret codes to transmit information. The American government asked a group of Navajo soldiers to develop a special code based on their unwritten language, which very few non-Navajos could speak or understand. The group became known as the Navajo Code Talkers.

The Navajo Code Talkers played an invaluable role in winning the war against the Japanese. However, their work was kept a secret for a long time, and it was not until many years later that they received any recognition for their contributions.

Joseph Bruchac

Bruchac said some books can take many years to complete. He worked on *Jim Thorpe's Bright Path* and *Jim Thorpe, Original All-American* for two decades.

Bruchac and his son Jim have coauthored several books. Bruchac said:

> Jim writes a draft and gives it to me. I read through it, revise it, and give it back to him. He reads it and we work out a final draft. Then we send it to our editor. It's a great process.

Bearwalker is the fifth novel in a series that includes *Skeleton Man*, *The Return of Skeleton Man*, *Whisper in the Dark*, and *The Dark Pond*.

Bruchac said:

What was fun about *Bearwalker* is that it takes
place in the Adirondacks and is based on a
hunting camp where my dad used to go. The main
character is an undersized kid who is a little like
me at that age. He goes to the camp to learn about
nature, and everything goes wrong. However,
when the monster bear threatens the people, it is
the boy who had always listened to the stories who
defeats the monster.

Bruchac said that traditional Native American
stories use monsters to teach that life is sometimes
threatening and it is important to be aware of the
dangers. Traditional stories also show that even
a small person can defeat or escape a monster
if he does the right thing. People can turn to
the traditional story for guidance and recipes for
survival. "All human beings have the capability
for doing that which is positive and that which is
negative," he said. "Everybody has within them the
twisted mind and the good mind. *Gah-neh-go-hi-yo*
means 'the good mind.'"

Award-Winning Books

Joseph Bruchac's books have won many awards. Here are just a few of them.

Hidden Roots
- American Indian Youth Literature Award, 2006

Jim Thorpe's Bright Path
- Carter G. Woodson Award, 2005

Skeleton Man
- School Library Journal Best Books, 2002

The Winter People
- School Library Journal Best Books, 2002

The Heart of a Chief
- Jane Addams Children's Book Honor Book Award, 1999

Dog People
- Paterson Prize for Children's Literature, 1997

Four Ancestors: Stories, Songs, and Poems from Native North America
- Skipping Stones Award, 1997

The Boy Who Lived with the Bears: And Other Iroquois Stories
- Boston Globe Horn Book Honor Award, 1996

Keepers of the Earth: Native American Stories and Environmental Activities for Children (with Michael J. Caduto)
- ALA Best Books for Young Adults, 1990

Other Awards and Honors
- Empire State Award for Excellence in Literature to Young People, 2007
- Virginia Hamilton Literary Award, 2005
- National Education Association Civil Rights Award, 2003
- Lifetime Achievement Award from the Native Writers Circle of the Americas, 1999
- Writer of the Year Award and Storyteller of the Year Award from the Wordcraft Circle of Native Writers and Storytellers, 1998

Ktsi Nwaskw: Great Spirit

Bruchac and his wife live in a small cabin in Porter Corners, seven miles from the house he grew up in. He rises early and begins each day with karate exercises and stretching. Then he sits down at his computer and writes at least two or three pages. "I really get involved in the writing," he said. "Everything else disappears. If I'm working on revisions, I'll go into my study at ten o'clock at night and work until midnight or later."

He said:

I think writing comes to me from many different directions. I can wake up in the morning with an entire song in my head, go into my study, and write it down. If I don't write it down I might forget it, because so many things come to me like that. It's almost like the writing chooses me and says, "You must write me now." Because I have a good memory and I have been fortunate to have led a very full life thus far, there is so much I can draw upon in any given circumstance. I don't know where it comes from. I'm just glad it makes itself available to me. I don't have to know what makes it work, I am just glad it does. It is a great mystery. That mystery is beyond the understanding of human beings. The words in Abenaki for the creator or the creation force are *Ktsi Nwaskw*, or Great Spirit.

When Bruchac completes a chapter, Carol reads it and gives him suggestions. Once a month, Bruchac gathers with a group of other writers who share their writing with each other. He usually completes a manuscript before showing it to his editor.

He said:

I think it is important for young readers to know that writers benefit from editors. Every editor I've had has improved my work and has helped me see what I might not have seen on my own. An editor does not make me change the content or the truth of a story, but I may have to change the phrasing or the focus to make it work better. An editor can see the extra words, the unnecessary details, and the places where things need filling in.

Joseph Bruchac with his wife, Carol, in front of Bowman's Store and the house he grew up in.

Bruchac enjoys talking with young people about writing. He advises them to be happy with who they are and reminds them that great things are ahead. "I honestly think that when you live widely and deeply, you are able to write better," he said. "You can draw on those things you have learned, but you can't do it quickly."

Bruchac explained that in Native and traditional cultures around the world, the elderly are celebrated as those who keep the memory of the people. The elders wear their white hair like a badge of honor.

Ndakinna Wilderness Center

"My son Jim started the Ndakinna Wilderness Center over a decade ago," said Bruchac.

Ndakinna means "our land." The goal of the center is to teach awareness of the natural world in a respectful way, as well as traditional skills like animal tracking, wilderness survival, and fire making. It is located on the ninety acres, now a nature preserve, that my grandparents gave to my father and mother. My mother passed the property on to Jim and Jesse in her will.

Joseph Bruchac

When deer run through the forest, they signal each other by lifting their tails. The bottom of the tail is white, and they follow each other's tails as they would follow a white flag.

So, too, the white hair of the elder is a signal that we must turn to them and listen. I see myself in the role of an uncle, passing on to someone else's children those things I would want my children to know and understand, and to do it as honorably, as truthfully, and as interestingly as possible. I continue doing the work and try to do the best I can. I just hope to tell a good story and touch a few people in a good way.

44

Selected Books
by Joseph Bruchac

Picture Books
- *Between Earth and Sky*
- *A Boy Called Slow*
- *Crazy Horse's Vision*
- *The Earth Under Sky Bear's Feet*
- *The First Strawberries*
- *The Great Ball Game*
- *How Chipmunk Got His Stripes* (with Jim Bruchac)
- *Many Nations: An Alphabet of Native America*
- *Squanto's Journey*
- *Thirteen Moons on Turtle's Back* (with Jonathan London)
- *Turtle's Race with Beaver* (with Jim Bruchac)

Fiction
- *Arrow Over the Door*
- *Buffalo Song*
- *Children of the Longhouse*
- *Dawn Land*
- *Dog People*
- *Eagle Song*
- *Geronimo*
- *The Girl Who Helped Thunder* (with Jim Bruchac)
- *The Heart of a Chief*
- *Keepers of the Earth* (with Michael Caduto)
- *March Toward the Thunder*
- *Native American Games and Stories* (with Jim Bruchac)
- *Pocahantas*
- *Sacajawea*
- *Skeleton Man*
- *Turtle Meat and Other Stories*
- *The Way*
- *The Winter People*

Collections of Traditional Stories
- *The Boy Who Lived With the Bears*
- *The Faithful Hunter*
- *The Girl Who Married the Moon* (with Gayle Ross)
- *Native American Stories*
- *Pushing Up the Sky: Seven Plays for Children*
- *When the Chenoo Howls* (with Jim Bruchac)
- *The Wind Eagle*

Nonfiction
- *Bowman's Store: A Journey to Myself*
- *Seeing the Circle*

Abenaki (ah-ben-AH-kee)—An American Indian group of northern New England and Quebec.

Algonquian—An American Indian group of the Ottowa River valley.

Chiricahua—An American Indian group of Arizona; part of the Apache Nation.

descent—Having ancestors from a particular country or ethnicity.

heritage—Something handed down from earlier generations or the past.

multicultural—Having elements from many different cultures.

naturalist—One who studies the natural world, especially animals and plants.

Onondaga—An American Indian group of New York and Canada.

paternal—On the father's side.

stereotype—An attitude or idea toward a person or group that is oversimplified or prejudiced.

welfare—The well-being of others.

Joseph Bruchac
with Michelle
Parker-Rock

Books

Bruchac, Joseph. *Bowman's Store: A Journey to Myself*. New York: Lee & Low Books, 2001.

Bruchac, Joseph. *Seeing the Circle*. Katonah, N.Y.: R.C. Owen Publishers, 1999.

Drew, Bernard A. *100 More Popular Young Adult Authors: Biographical Sketches and Bibliographies*. Westport, Conn.: Libraries Unlimited, 2002.

Internet Addresses

Joseph Bruchac's Home Page
<http://www.josephbruchac.com>

James Bruchac's Home Page
<http://www.jamesbruchac.com>

The Ndakinna Education Center
<http://www.ndakinnacenter.org>

Index

A

Abenaki Indians, 6, 8, 9, 12–13, 18, 25, 30, 36, 42

American Indians (Native Americans), 6, 8, 9–10, 11–13, 18, 22, 24–26, 28, 29, 31–32, 34–37, 39, 42, 43

B

Bowman Bruchac, Flora Marion (mother), 6, 7, 8, 9, 18, 25, 29, 44

Bowman, Jesse (grandfather), 6, 7–9, 11–12, 13, 14, 17, 18, 21, 22, 24, 27, 35, 37, 44

Bowman's Store, 8, 13, 16, 27

Bruchac, James (son), 8, 27, 29–30, 33, 38, 44

Bruchac, Jesse (son), 28, 29–31, 33, 44

Bruchac, Joseph
  advice to writers, 42–43
  childhood, 6–10, 11–17
  education, 13, 15, 16–19, 20–24, 26
  as naturalist, 15–16, 17, 19, 22

as storyteller, 28, 29–30, 32–33

teaching career, 26–27, 28

writing career and methods, 16, 17, 22, 23–24, 26, 27–28, 30–32, 36–39, 40, 41–44

Bruchac, Joseph (grandfather), 8

Bruchac, Joseph Jr. (father), 7, 9, 10, 18–19, 25, 26, 44

Bruchac, Margaret (sister), 7

Bruchac, Mary Ann (sister), 7

C

Caduto, Michael, 31, 40

Cornell University, 19, 20–22

D

Dennis, Maurice, 25

Dunham Bowman, Marion Flora (grandmother), 6, 7–9, 11, 13, 15, 17, 18

Dunham, Ed, 6

Dunham, Flora, 6

F

Fadden, Jon Kahionhes, 31

Fadden, Ray, 25, 29

Furlong, Tommy, 21

G

Ghana, 26–27

Gill, John, 30

H

Hrdlicka, Pauline (grandmother), 8

L

London, Jonathan, 31–32

N

Navajo Code Talkers, 37, 38

Ndakinna Wilderness Center, 44

P

Paley, Grace, 24

Papineau, Alice (Dewasentah), 26

Phillips, David, 21, 22

Powhatan, 25

Pray, Leon, 10

S

Skidmore College, 14, 28

Swift Eagle, 25, 29

Syracuse University, 23–24

W

Worthen Bruchac, Carol (wife), 22, 27, 28, 42